INTRUSION

GOOGLE
STREETVIEW

CALAIS
FRANCE

2014–2018

GOOGLE STREETVIEW

CALAIS
FRANCE

2019

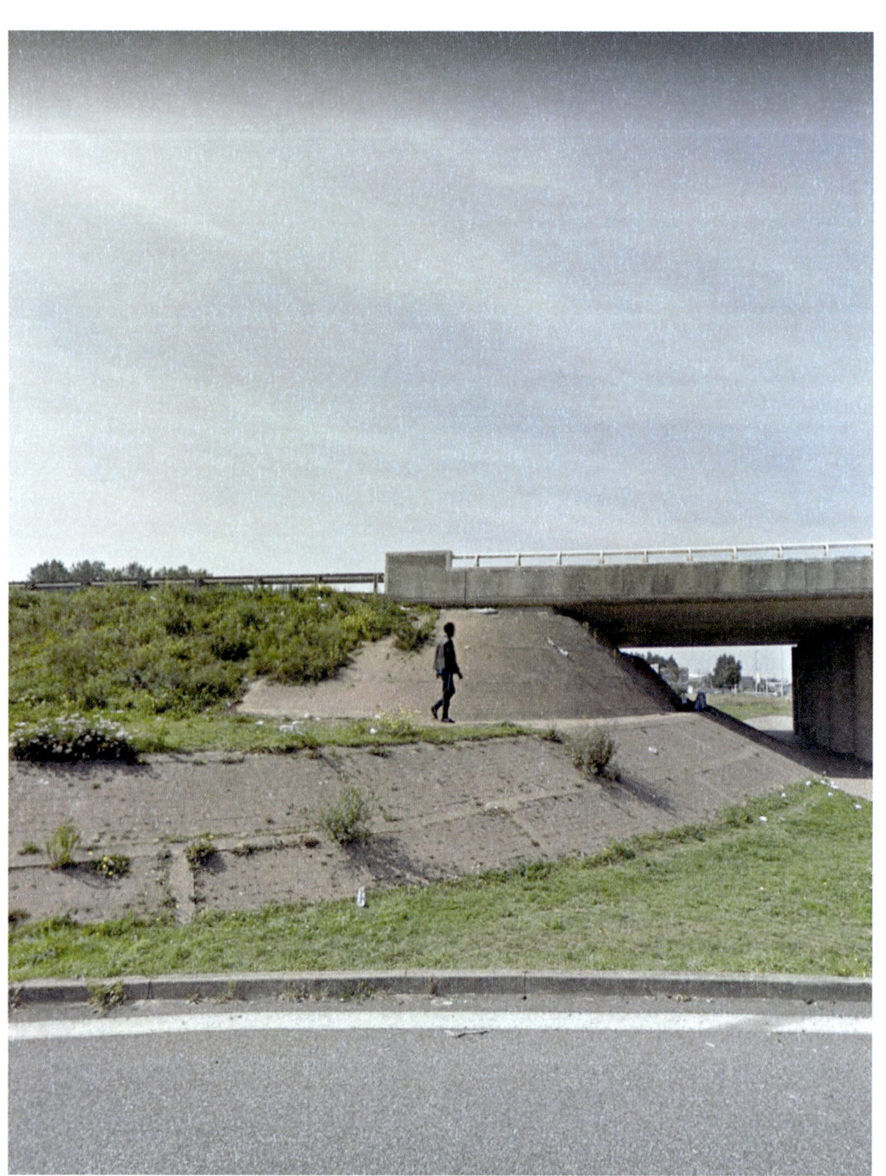

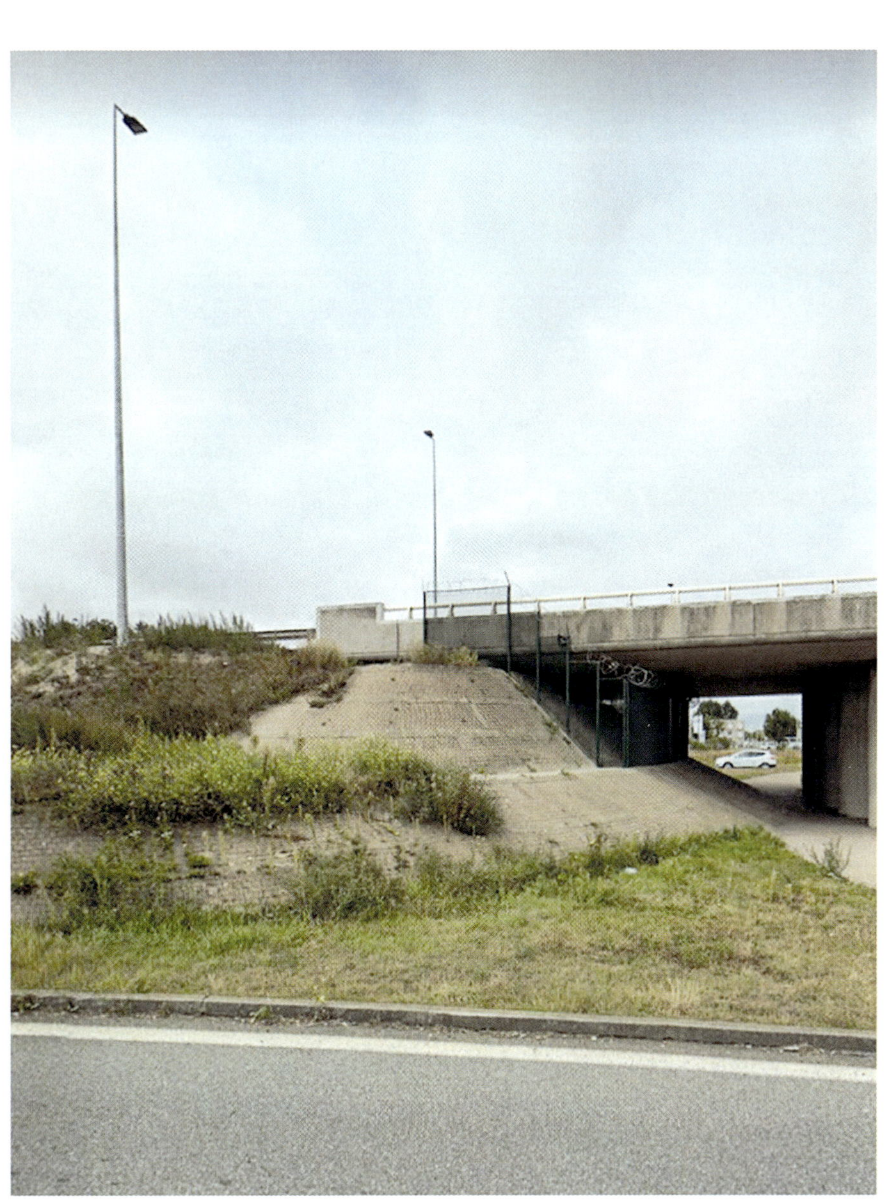

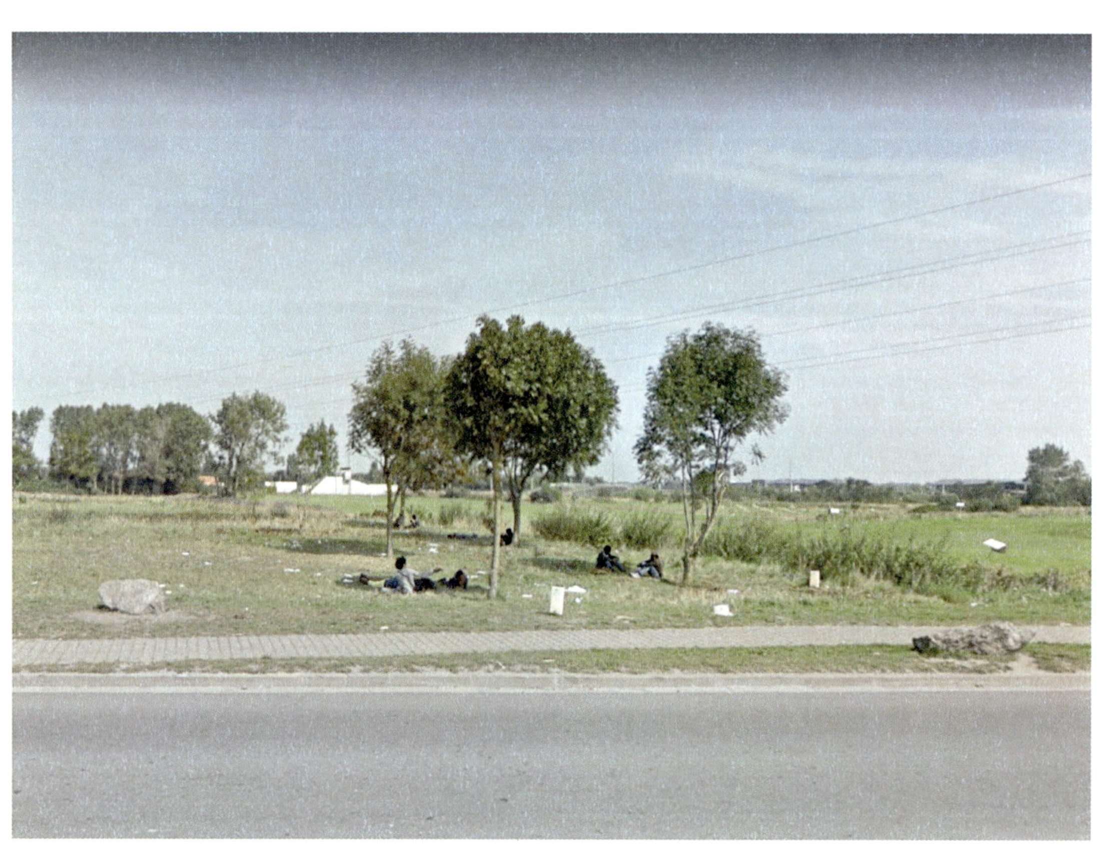

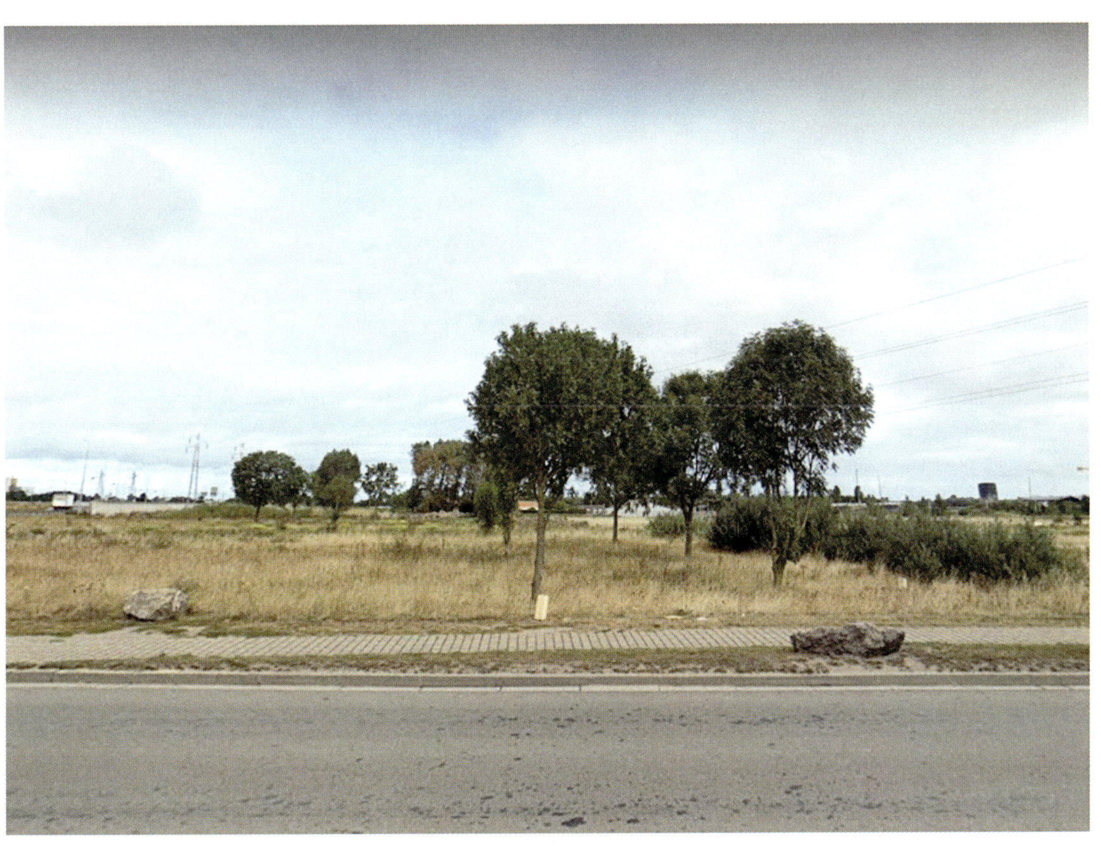

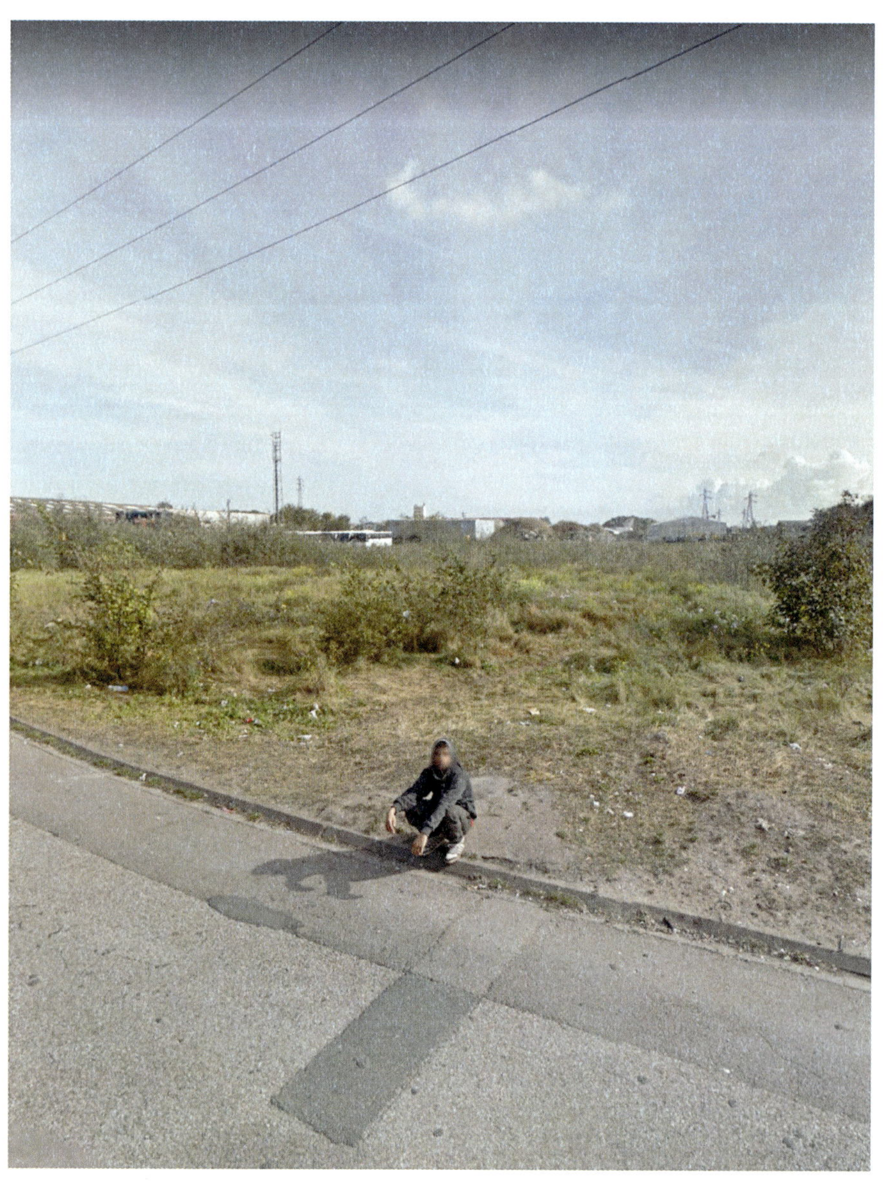

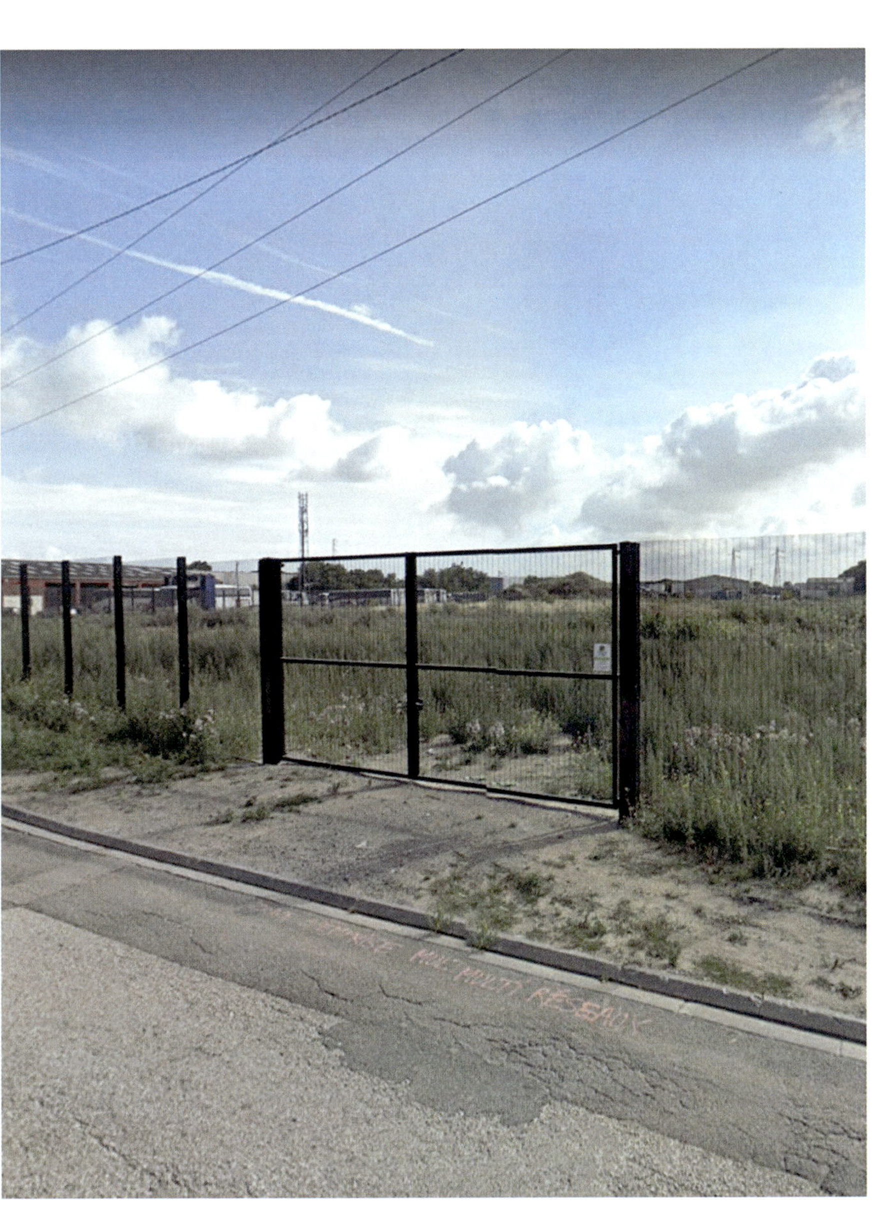

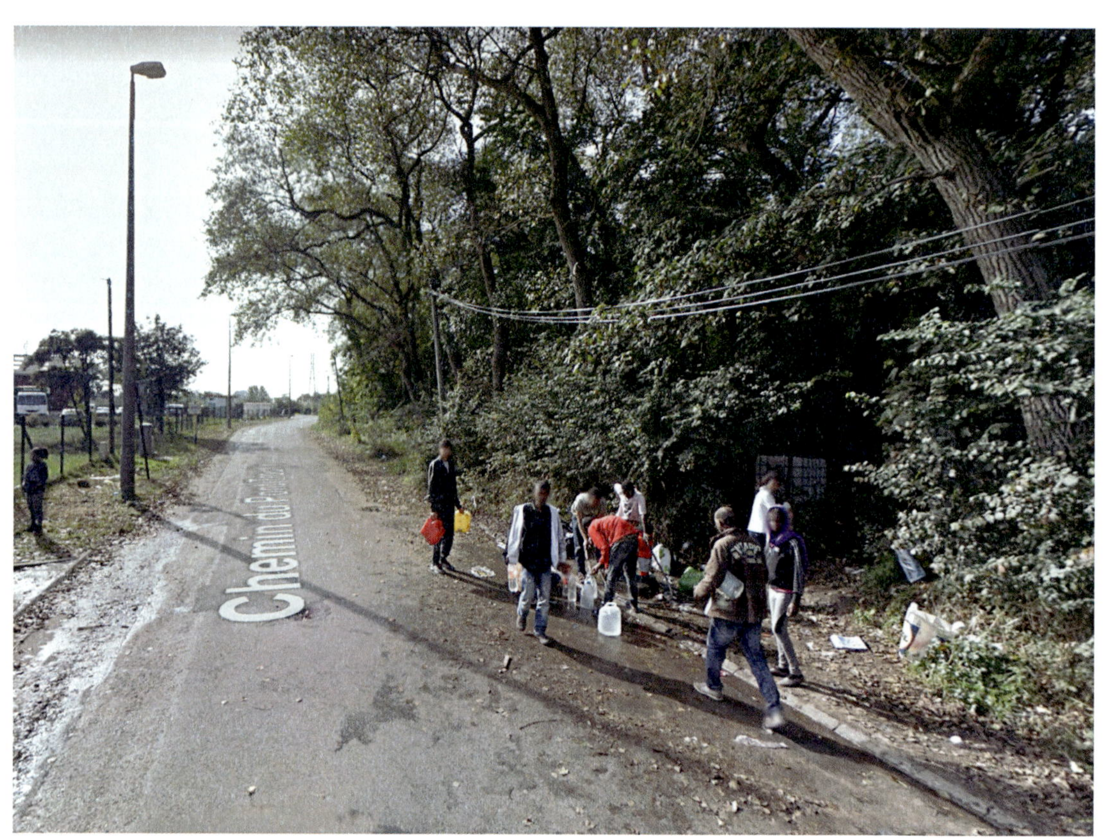

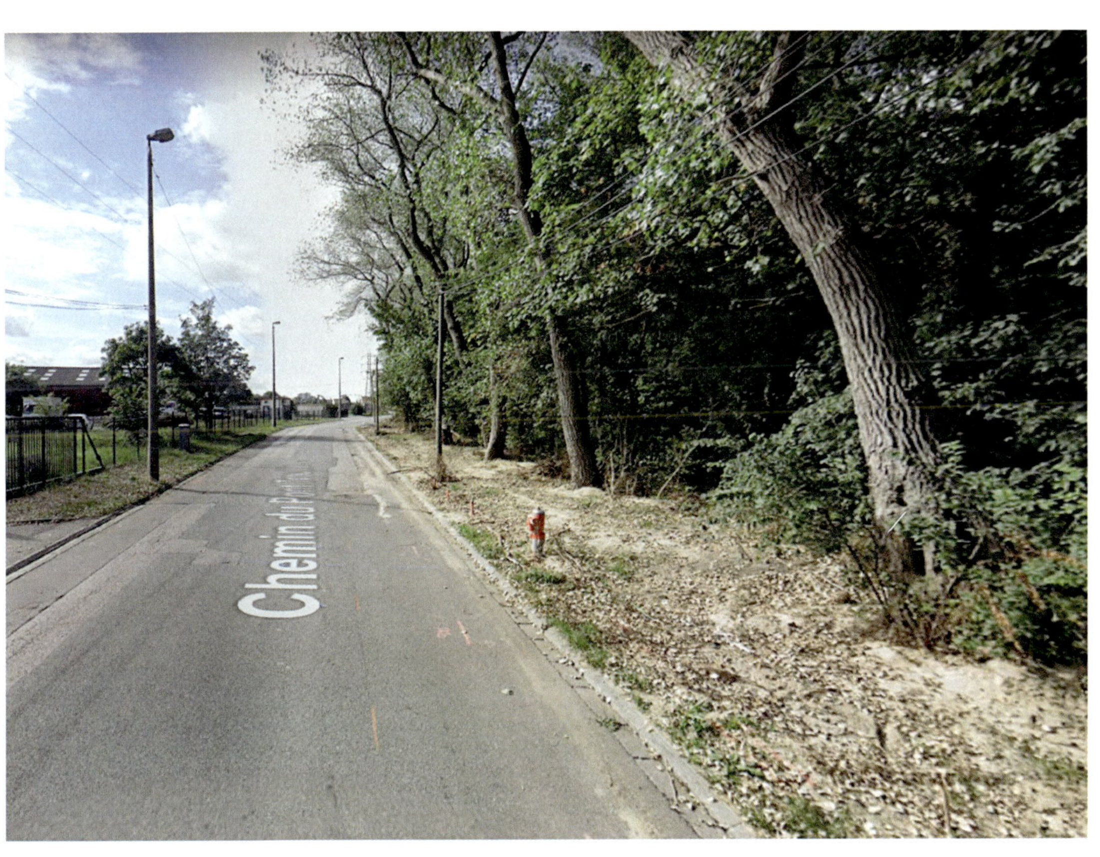
Chemin du

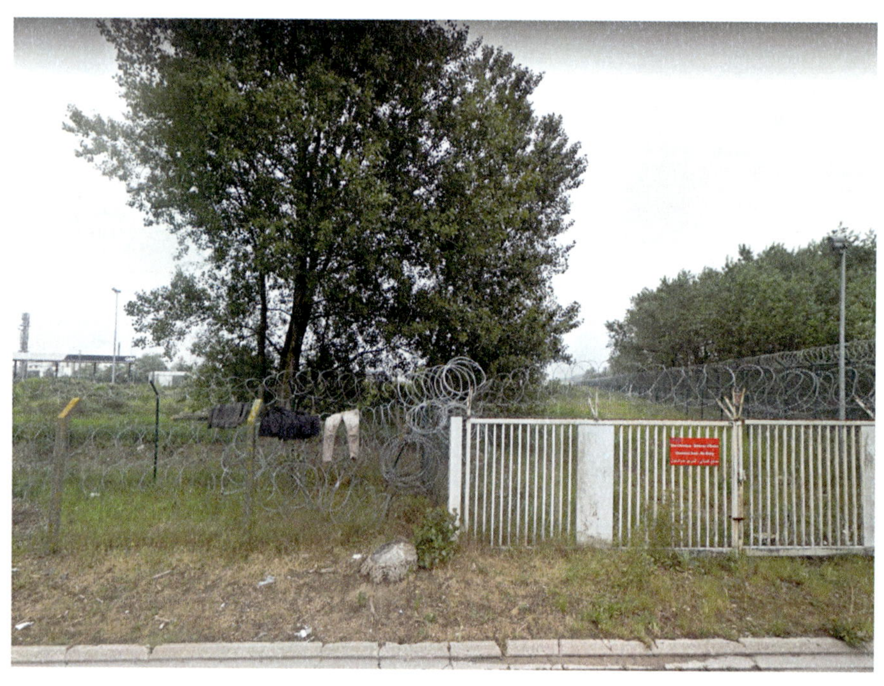

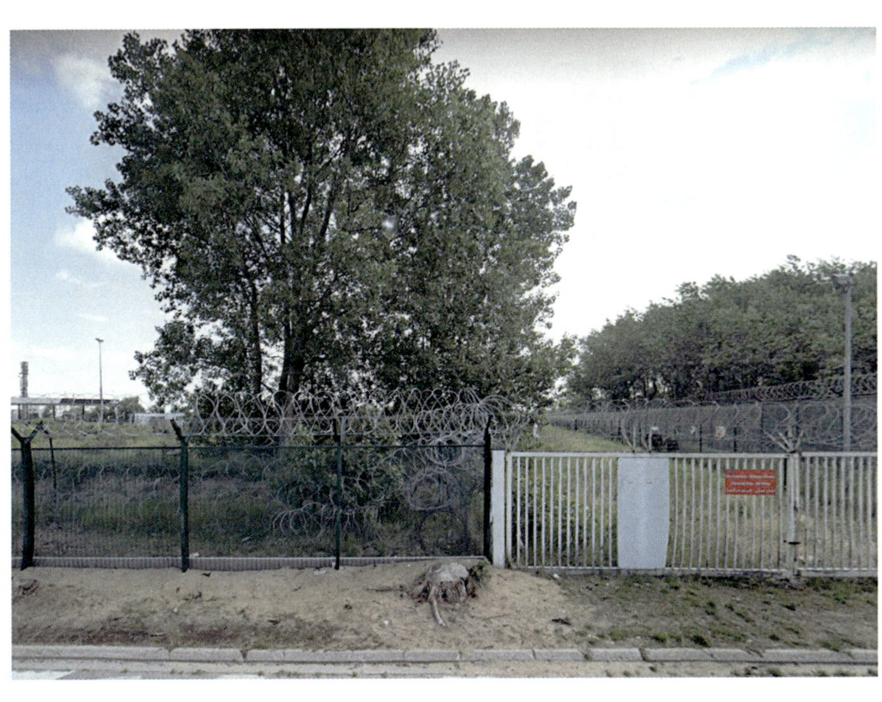

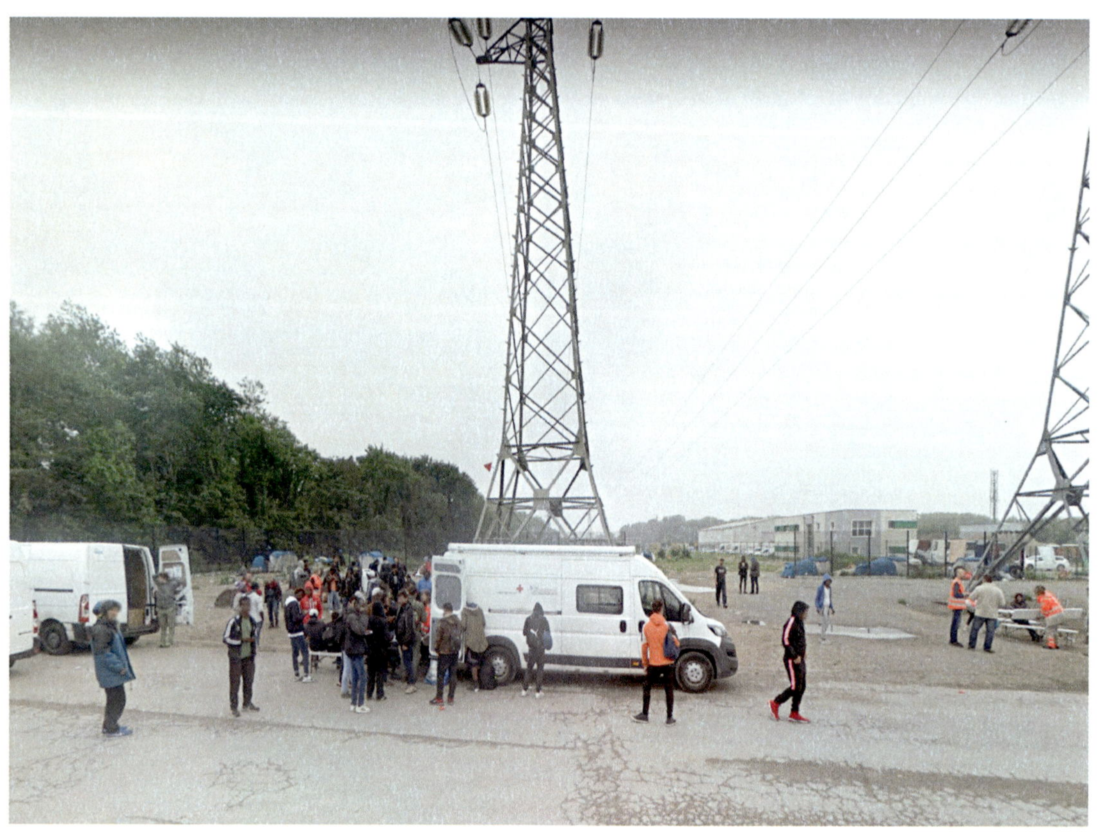

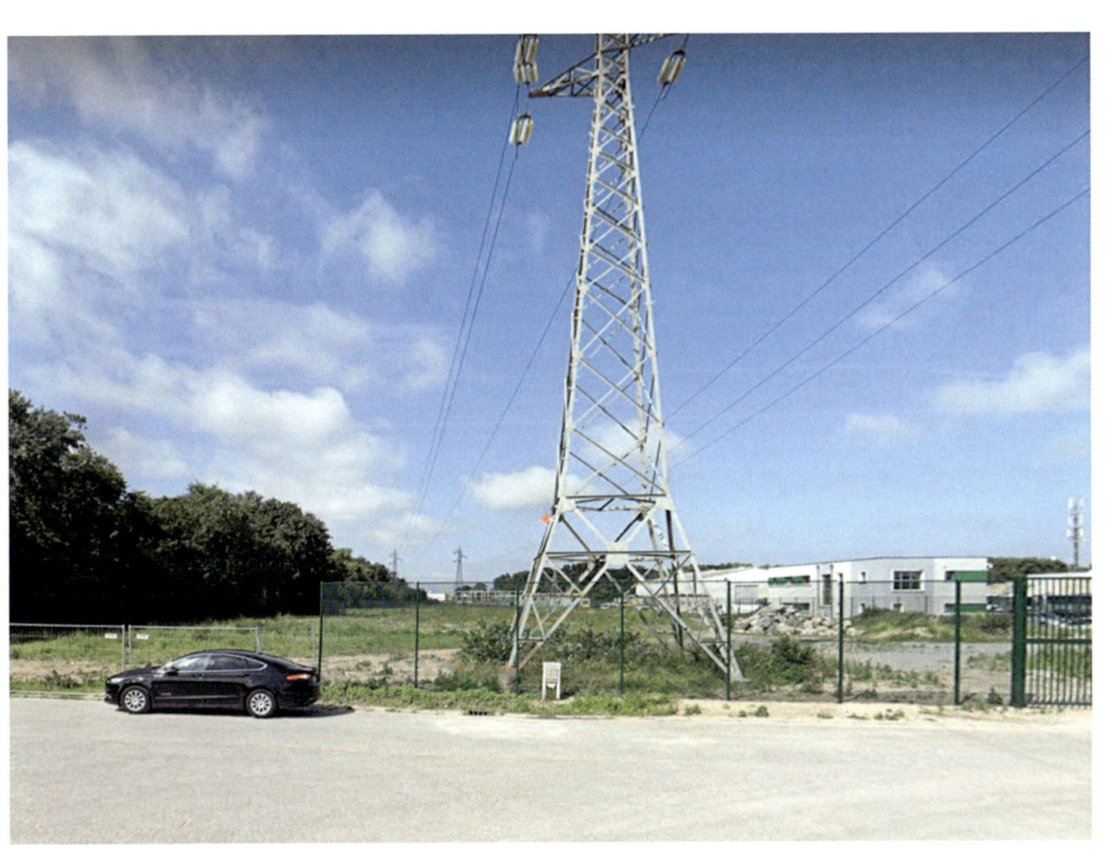

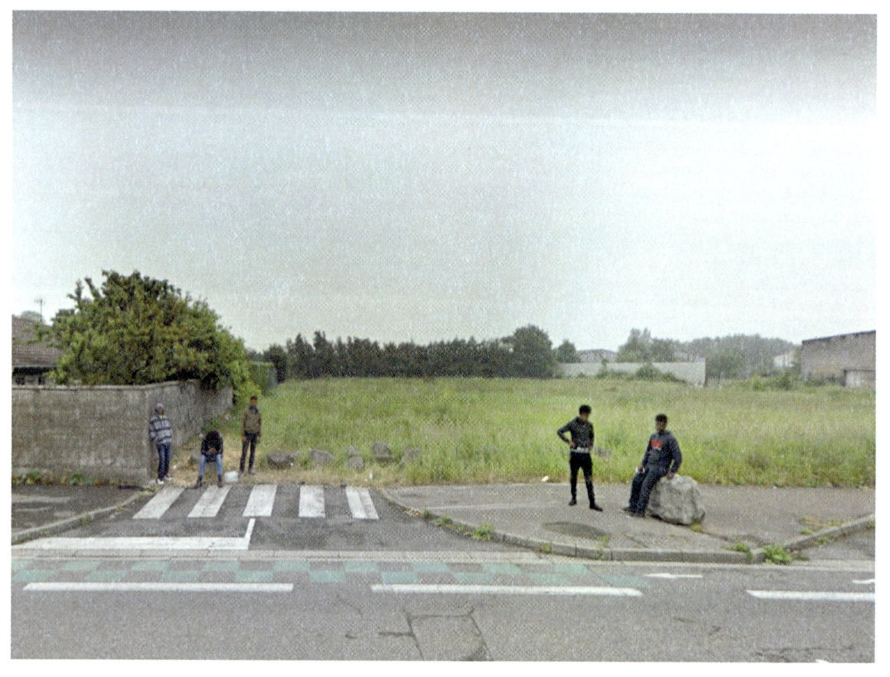

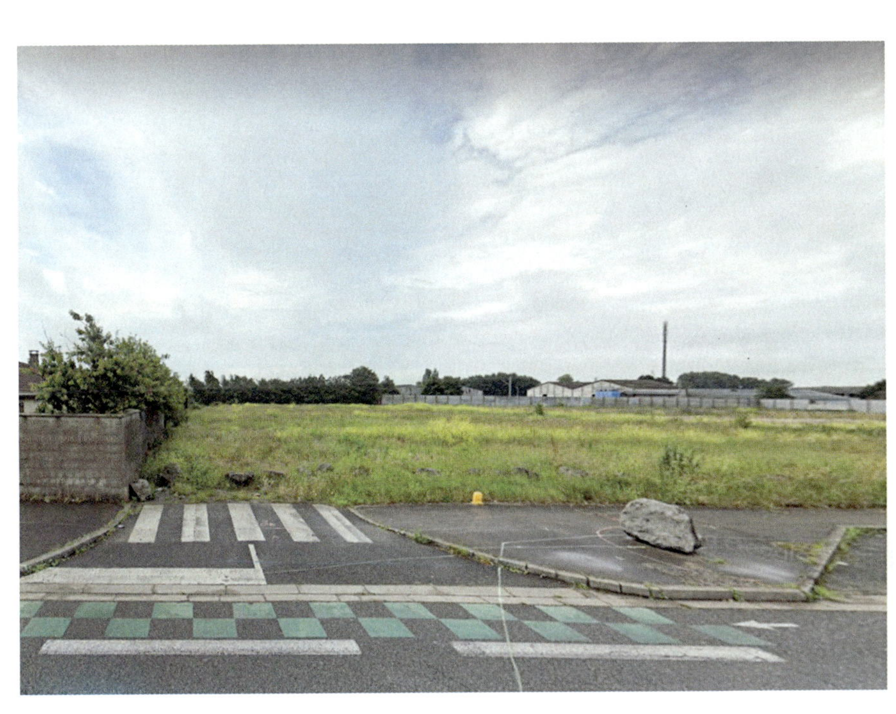

MAPPING
ETHICO-AESTHET

Unlawful intrusions[10] cut through and across our maps; they cannot be prevented. Lines of loose ends and erratic beginnings,[9] which both present and challenge traces of flight. We perceive independent rhythms with their own dynamics, sometimes set off by us, now snapping back in a kind of panic, then seeming to combine at random, forming chaotic polyphonies. A new mode is inherent in the catastrophes, crises, rapid upheavals, and transformations which have overcome us: the realization that even escape is escaping something else, even catastrophe is haunted by catastrophe, so that alterity can break in at any moment. Instability, fragility, and volatility are now givens. Ruins are now our homeland.[14] Precarity weighs on us, even if we feel ourselves to be in safety. As well as the insurmountable indeterminacy of all that is, we are confronted with the unpredictability of events, which are indifferent to everything already in existence, and which cannot be used to justify any particular action. Hopes and perspectives are dashed, questions of responsibility are rebuffed.[13] Nonetheless, we can be surprised by life in the midst of this rubble, its fragile temporary assemblages: a life in the shadows, in the gaps, at the margins. The world is ironic. The world, for better or worse, is a trickster. In the ruins of our struggles, there is neither a way forward nor a way back, continuity and discontinuity hang in the balance. The only possibility left is to hook into heterogeneous forces of proliferating multiplicity. Perhaps in this way we can allow the intimacy of intrusion to take place.

Maps draw t
Map-making is
Ways of cartograph
In both discursive and sensory terms,
sounds, and stories. We can live in, thr
er sense, a map creates a resonance bet
neous force relationships. In this way, it
of a concrete structure, acquiring conti
a map, everything existing can be seen
graphic center of vibration: What are
tors, individuals, ideologies, and world
connect or predetermine? Which ones
be viewed as a map: a term or concept, a
a simple gesture, a children's book, a set
social media, narratives of our dreams,
itself. All things embody transversal
event-constellations. But what should
(modernist, capitalist, Western, metap
tives which promised stable endpoints
events, which have happened and whic
reconciled with the basic realities of life
responsible for a planetary crisis? Ho

conducted when they jeopardize individual lives, and ultimately undermine the shared basis for all our lives? If we take s
structures which try to keep intrusive questions at bay. Questions of what is given value, why, when and for whom? We n
phy, on the other hand, would focus on the fragility of its modeling systems. It would be attentive to possible losses throu
quirements would emerge as part of these new forms of cartography. The following five suggestions should help to promp
unstable, our making of representations should be transformed into a space of encounter.[14] This encounter can emerge fr
gent efforts from a point of shared becoming; it includes learning to coalesce with the fluctuating processes of its emergen
can be re-organized and re-functionalized in diverse and unforeseen ways. 2. *Making ourselves pay attention:* Withir
selves pay attention.[13] Doing so could slow down these processes, putting them at our disposal, allowing us to better perc
bility of failed experiments. The aim would be to produce *new maps of noticing the possibilities of the indefinite* (without
ducible, no position can be developed without consideration of shared dependencies. Being considerate here means using
complexities should be left in place, in juxtaposition, they should be spread out before us.[3,11] This would mean different field
recognition of other ontologies, which have been created from different points of view. We might be able to perceive co
4. *Being accountable:* Bearing witness to the subaltern should not focus on representing the other or attempting to sp
possible consequences. Our responsibility is located in what our contingent constructions actually generate: the answers t
can become aware of *the maps which we create in order to create other maps.*[6] 5. *Learning to compose-with:* It should b
tion waiting, nor are there universal laws toward which we can strive. We need different narratives, which think in terms
cannot be easily or permanently linked together. This implies a practice more characterized by questions than answers, by
cartography: this might not ›succeed‹ in incorporating int

»What do you do when your world starts to fall apart?«[14]

»How do we build caring relationships

ITRUSION:
C CARTOGRAPHY

ther worlds.
orld-making.[6]
define ways of life.
ps contain graphics, diagrams, images,
gh and with these elements. In a broad-
en the unconnected noise of heteroge-
omponent parts can seem to form part
ity and contour. In this conception of
s having the characteristics of a carto-
jectories, paths, limits, categories, ac-
which it makes possible? Which does it
duce the existing itself? Anything can
object, a line, a point, a body, an image,
instructions, user interfaces, apps and
ars and hopes. Nothing abides within
s, as well as the possibility of future
done now, when the basic narratives
sical...) structuring our maps – narra-
ought about by necessary sequences of
continue to happen – can no longer be
And which indeed turn out to be partly
hould practices of materialization be

Almost imperceptibly, our maps are systematically subordinated to fixations, perspectives hermetically sealed to fend off intrusion, presumably in order to preserve themselves unchanged. Of course, this is a question of security, in other words, drawing boundaries of inclusion so as to keep multiplicity and randomness at bay. But what is still more perfidious about these calculated modes of representation is that they no longer simply create a center, which is then selectively cordoned off. In a way that is both complicated and flexible, heterogeneous value systems are translated and redirected, circulating according to algorithms dominated by economic expediency.[14] These chains of circulation are akin to labyrinths which have been cunningly locked: we can only get out by reentering at some other point.[4] Calculated methodology, through its goal-oriented maxims, subsumes all forces to global axiomatics, but pays no attention to the resources and creative conditions needed for accumulation to take place: »We cannot care about everything.« Maps are produced with all traces of their production rendered invisible, ultimately made to function smoothly, without controversy. Here, encounters with the alien are canceled out. The incommensurable is fitted into a uniform scale[6, 8, 14], an integrated whole. This gaze only accepts what corresponds to its own deceptive framework, with its evocation of accuracy and clarity. But purity promotes barrenness, domesticated lives within cramped monocultures. Then, when all breath has been finally extinguished, people move on with a shrug.

iously the new requirements of our time, the imperative task is to prevent a retreat into ever-deeper citadels, bubble-like
st also ask who or what remains excluded, suppressed or invisible through decisions that are made. Responsible cartogra-
exclusion and it would recognize vulnerable dependencies within our own material reality. A number of interrelated re-
eflections on this alternative kind of map-making: *1. Enabling encounter:* Where borders are uncertain and identities
the event of collaboration, bearing traces of alterity, and expand in unplanned ways. This includes thinking about diver-
. To remain open to unexpected events, we need a cartography which is not limited to individual perspectives, but which
ne forms of circulation which keep us in a condition of constant enchantment, we do not cultivate the art of making our-
e what is incompatible with them. There are risks which go along with this, including the risk of hesitation, and the possi-
ng stopped by the border guards of academic and other disciplines). *3. Being considerate:* Since the world seems irre-
form of judgment which – harking back to the original sense of *con-siderare* – acts together-with.[1] Contradictions and
re not separated over-hastily and thus dissolved. It would allow us to develop ways of thinking which incorporate a caring
licated patterns (*maps which map maps*) of interference which cause asymmetries to converge on a symmetrical matrix.
k on its behalf.[12] Instead, we should insist on being accountable[2] for our own creations, stand up publicly and accept the
y enable, whom they allow to come up with those answers, and the collectives toward which they point.[11] In this way, we
nderstood that this cannot be a question of conflict and harmony, or of resolution and stasis.[9] There is no great emancipa-
composition-with.[13] This process would be an unending one, an attempt to come to terms with entangled worlds which
ggestions than rules, aiming at the creative invention of *mutant coordinates.*[5] It presents the outline of an *ethico-aesthetic*
sions, but it might at least stage an encounter with them.

»whom
can we
not see
or grasp,
and what
are the
consequences
of such
selective
blindness?«[6]

ile recognizing divergent positions?«[11]

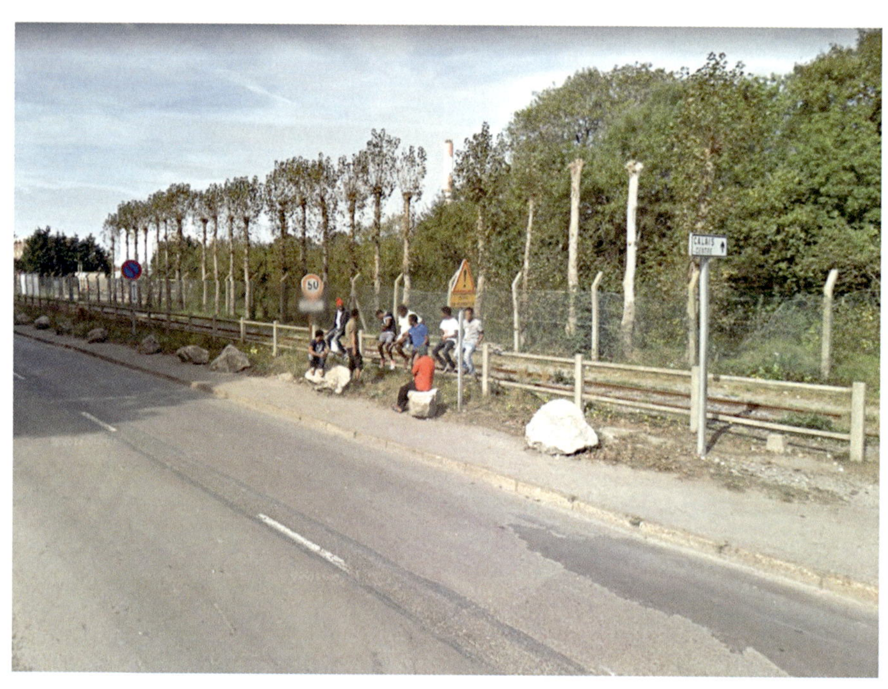
CALAIS
50

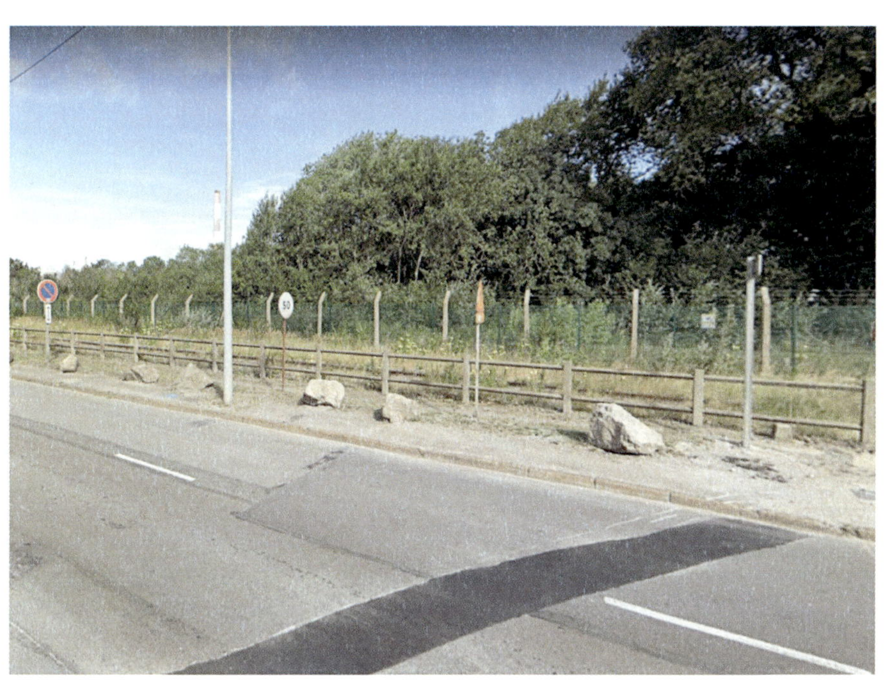
50

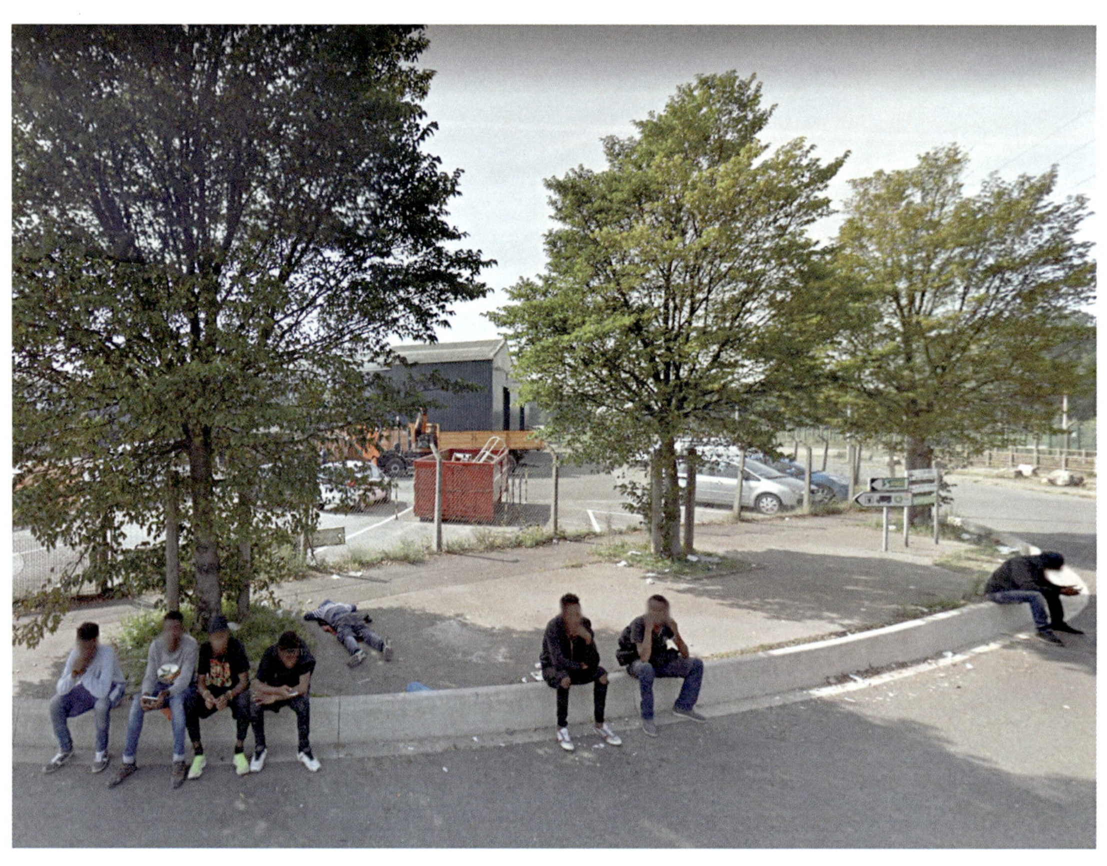

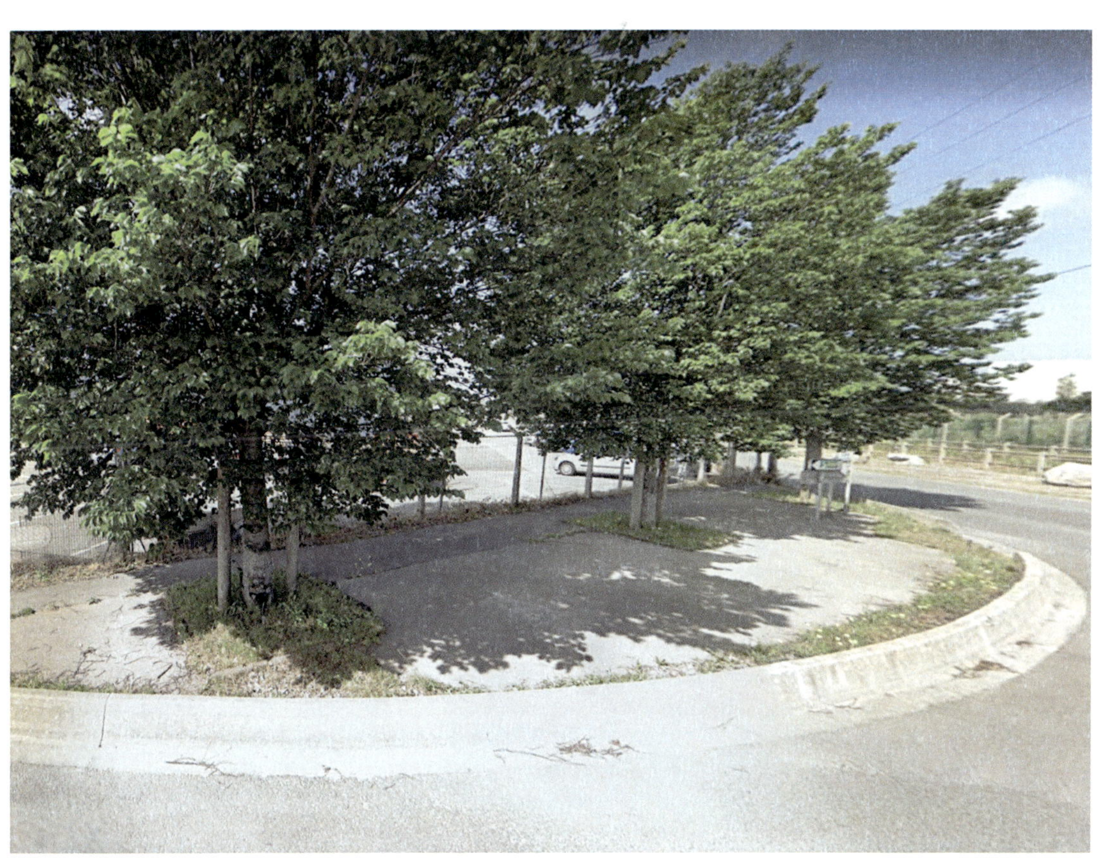

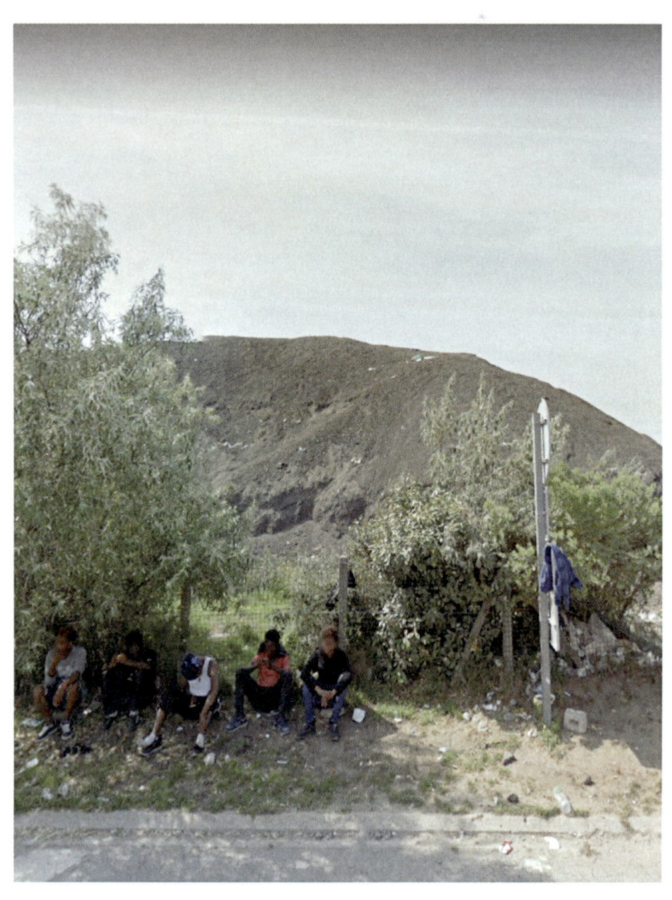

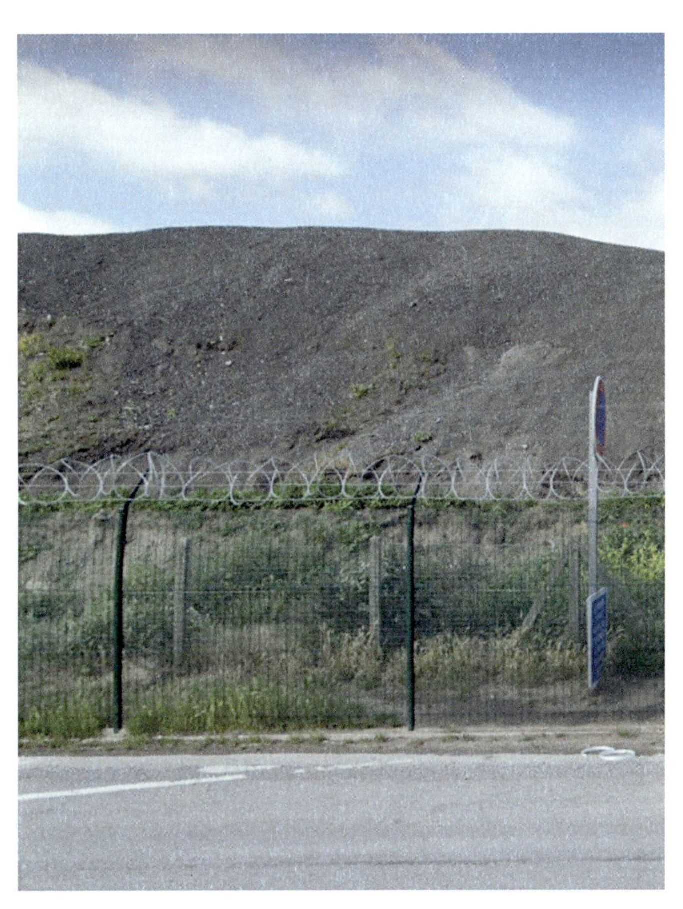

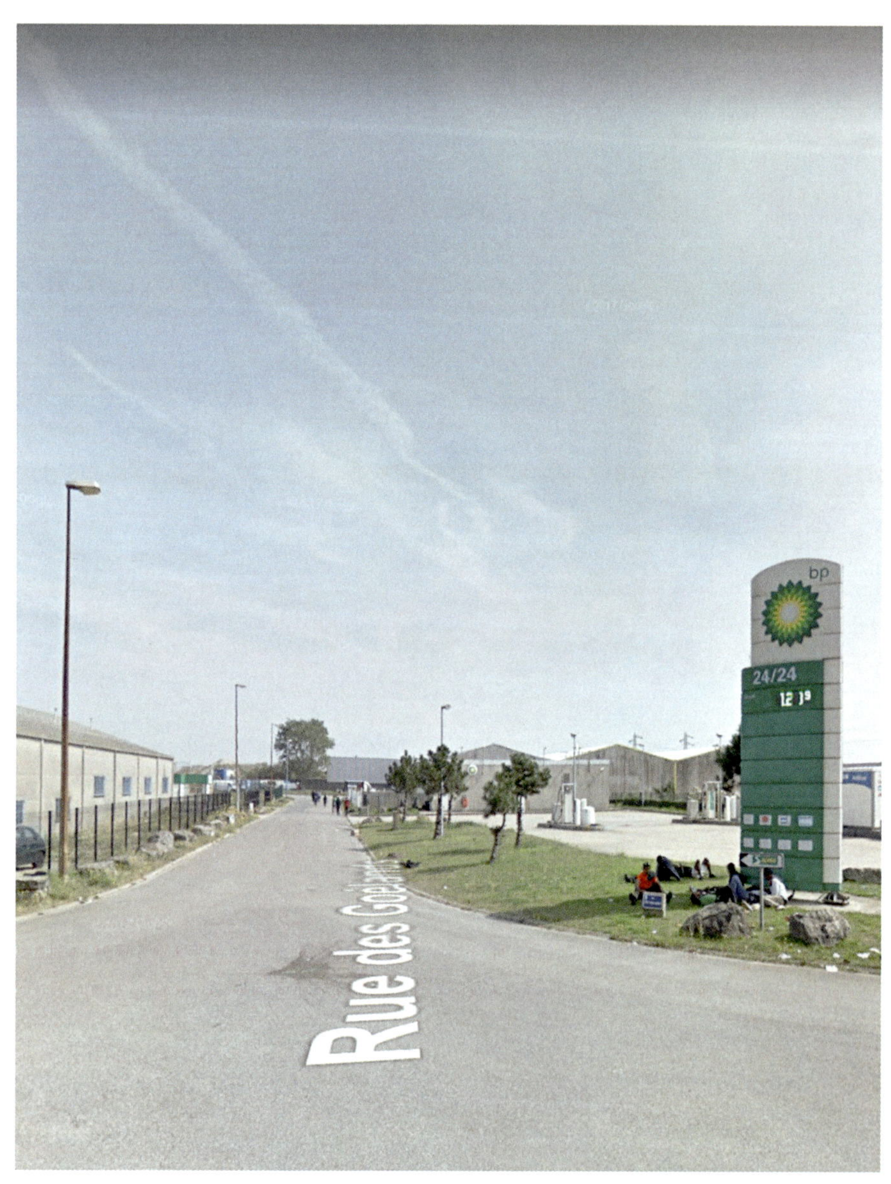
bp
24/24
Rue des

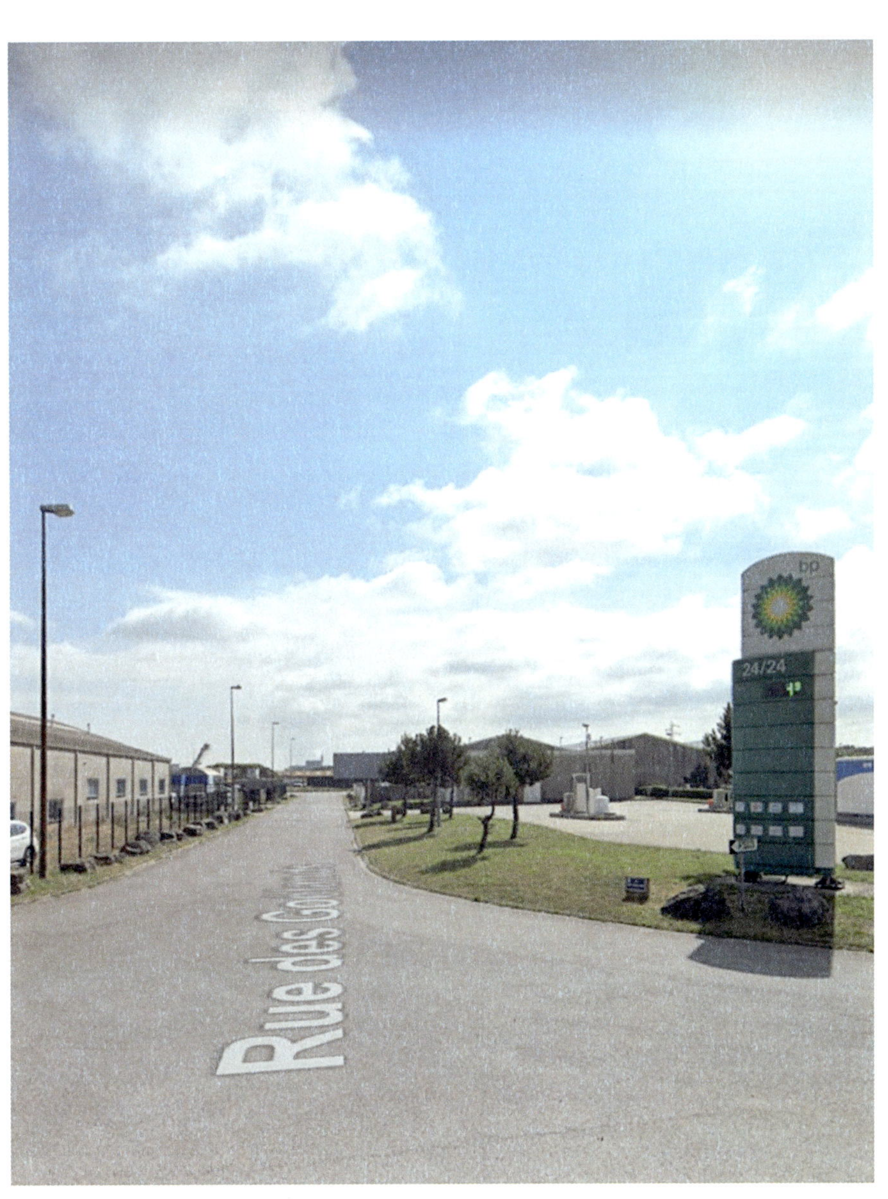
Rue des
bp
24/24

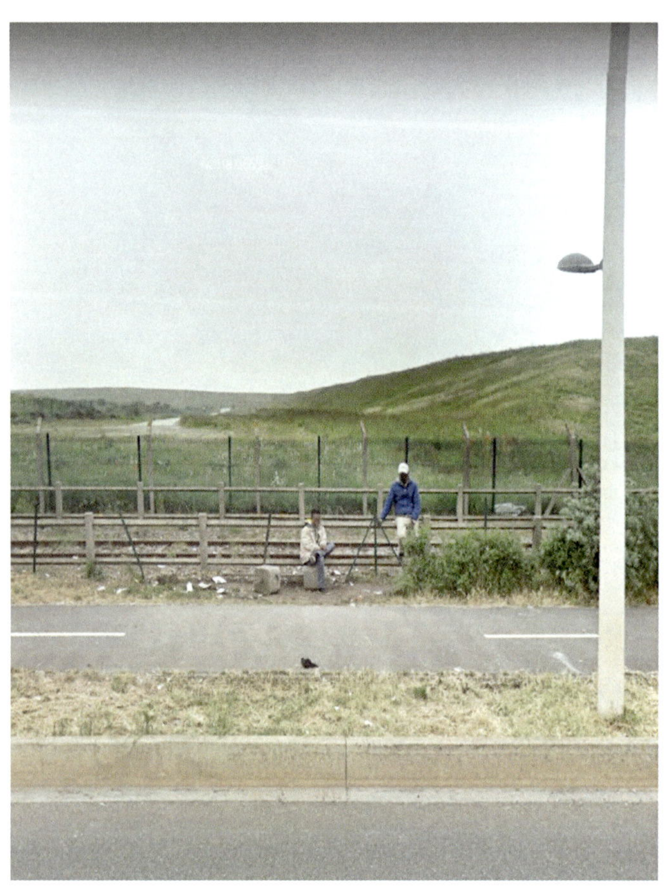

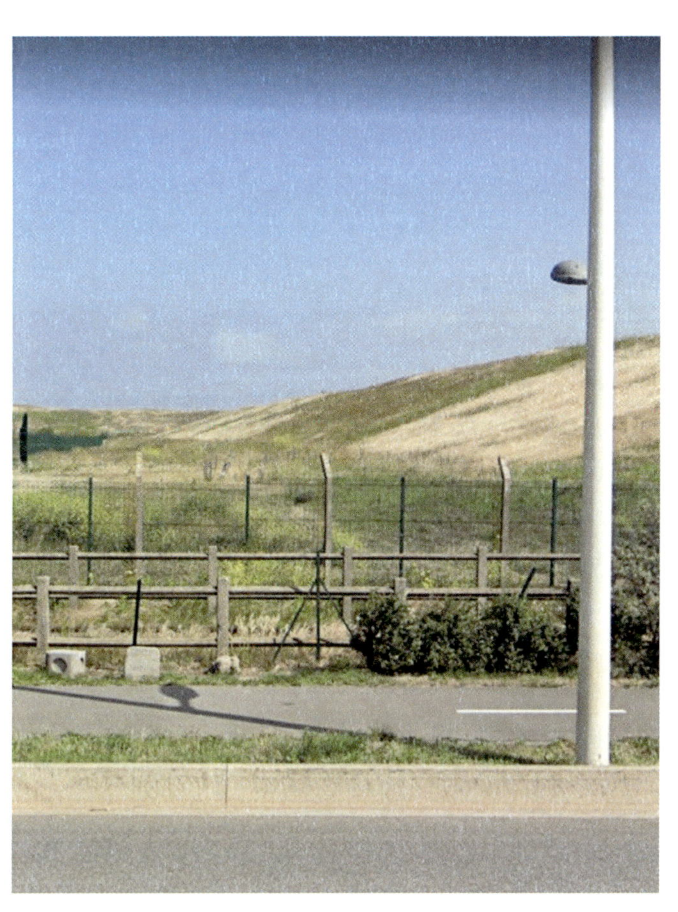

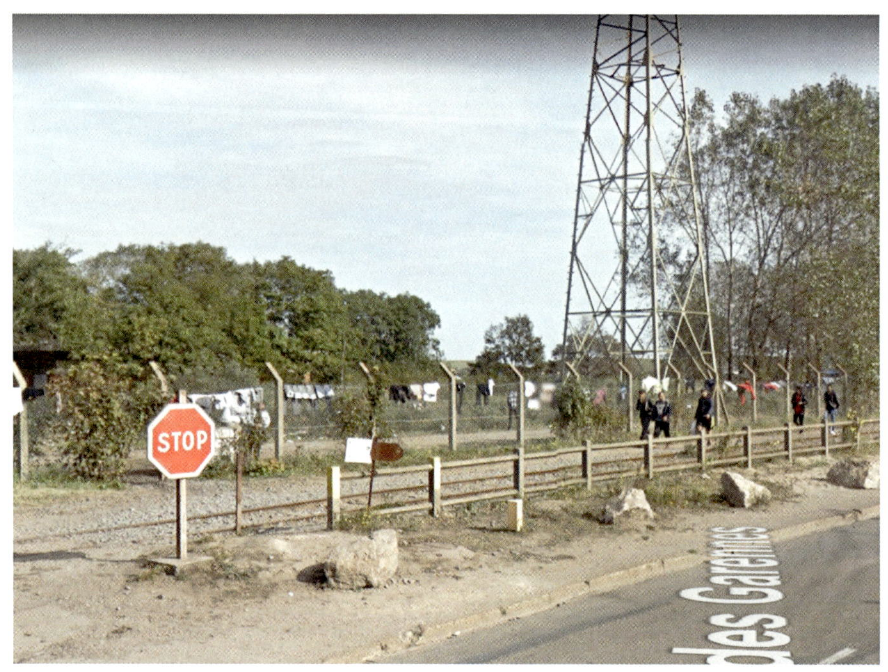
STOP
des Garennes

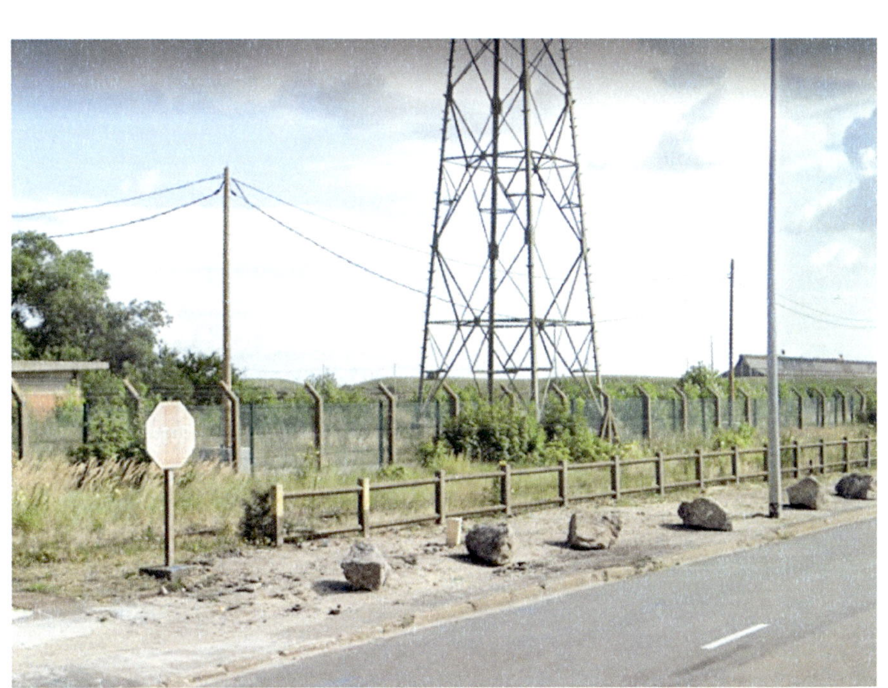

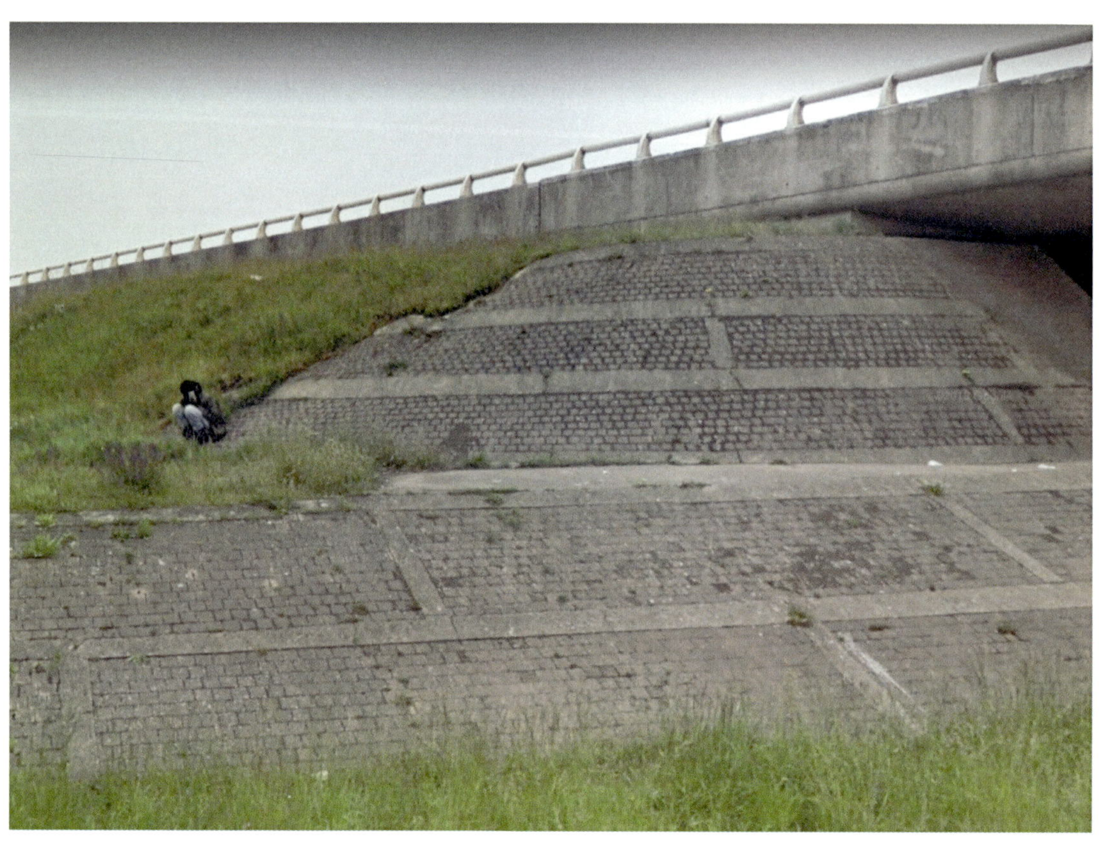

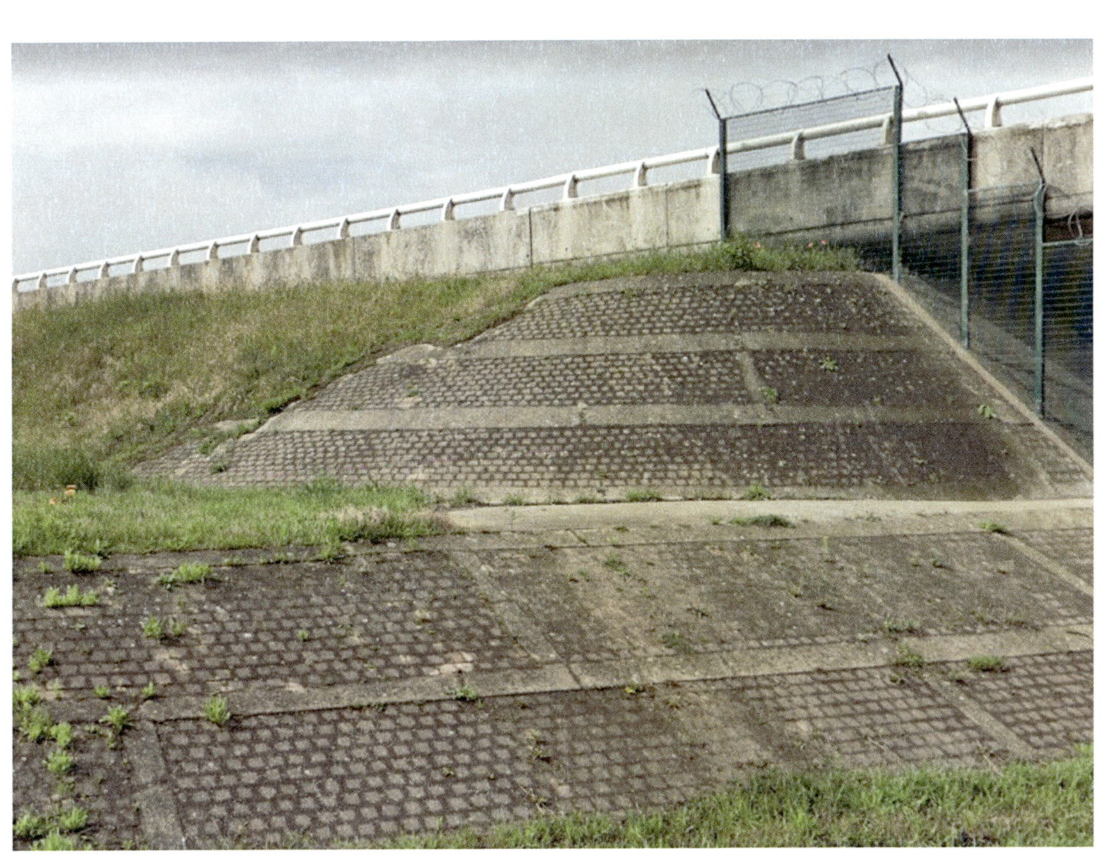

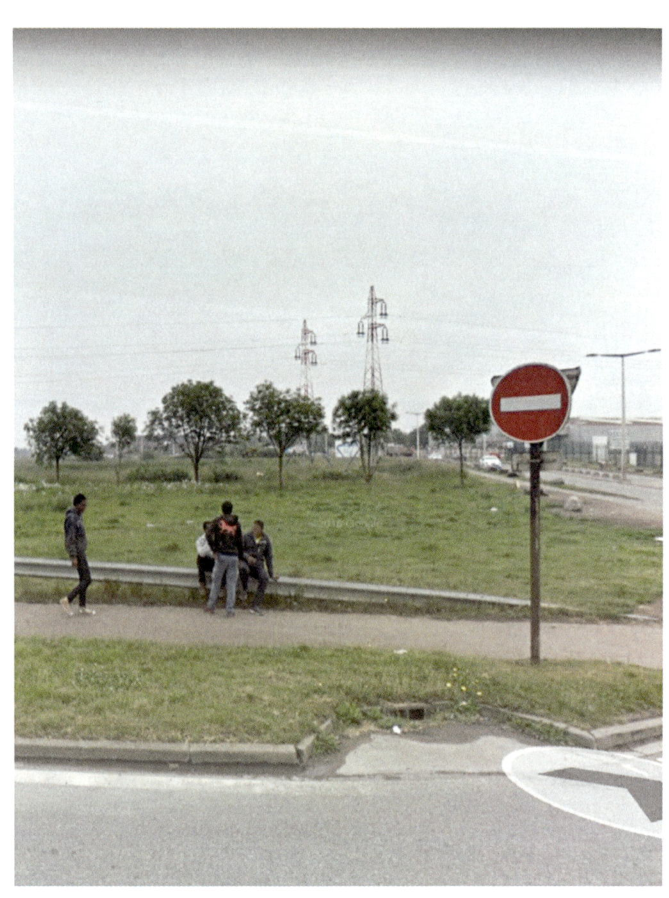

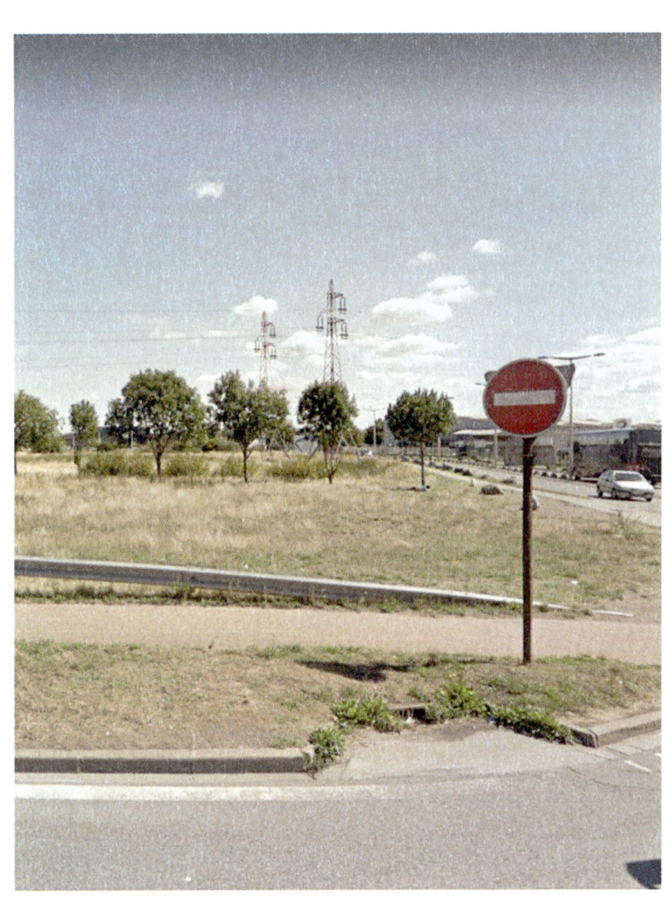

EPILOGUE AND FOOTNOTES

My text was written as part of the project by the artist Georg Lutz. Its relation to his work is not one of reception, nor of supplement, nor of introduction. Rather, this is a text of friendship. Concepts, forms and images emerge tentatively, in a process of interaction. Instead of passing mutual judgement, here these concepts, images, and forms encourage each other to speak. In Lutz's pairs of facing sculptures, illustrated on facing pages in this book, we can identify two contradictory modes, two speculative extremes, and – deriving from these – two different ways of narrating the contemporary world. These two opposed modes of narration are developed further in the facing textblocks of my own text. Lutz's work makes use of Google Maps photographs: Street View close-ups of the city of Calais in France, images which seem to contain a promise of ubiquitous realistic orientation. The autonomous life which Lutz finds in these images – and takes from them – manages to subvert Google's attempts at a purely objective cartographic practice, apparently closed and unresponsive to differential coincidences emerging at its margins. The unknown persons in the illustrations on the left – very likely refugees hoping to travel across the Channel to Britain[15] – are marginalized by the concrete fences shown in the pictures on the right, but also by the updates in Google Maps. Their story appears within a story: a cartographic gaze which can render them either visible or invisible. This discrepancy can be seen in Lutz's comparative analysis. His multi-temporal cartography takes place within other cartographies, and thus hints at a practice to which I want to make connections in my text.

Written together with:
[1]Arendt, Hannah: Some Questions of Moral Philosophy. [2]Barad, Karen: Meeting the Universe Halfway: Quantum Physics And the Entanglement of Matter And Meaning. [3]Braidotti, Rosi: Posthuman Knowledge. [4]Deleuze, Gilles and Félix Guattari: Anti-Oedipus: Capitalism and Schizophrenia. [5]Guattari, Félix: Chaosmosis: An Ethico-Aesthetic Paradigm. [6]Haraway, Donna: Modest_Witness@Second_Millennium.FemaleMan_Meets_OncoMouse: Feminism and Technoscience, New York 2018, 202. [7]King, Katie: Networked Reenactments: Stories Transdisciplinary Knowledges Tell, Durham & London 2011, 7. [8]Latour, Bruno: Paris: Invisible City. [9]Le Guin, Ursula: The Carrier Bag Theory of Fiction. [10]Nancy, Jean-Luc: L'Intrus, in: The New Centennial Review, Michigan, Volume 2, Number 3, Fall 2002, 1–14, 1. [11]Puig de la Bellacasa, Maria: Matters of Care: Speculative Ethics in More than Human Worlds, Minneapolis and London 2017, 83. [12]Spivak, Gayatri Chakravorty: Can the Subaltern Speak? [13]Stengers, Isabelle: In Catastrophic Times: Resisting the Coming Barbarism. [14]Tsing, Anna: The Mushroom at the End of the World: On the Possibility of Life in Capitalist Ruins, Princeton and Oxford 2015, 1.

[15]A text by Shumon T. Hussain also addresses Lutz's work on Calais, allowing us to follow this strand of entangled stories and weave them back into a wider whole: »The powerful photographs of the Calais ›Jungles‹ and the essayistic film documentary Ocean by Georg Lutz sketch the possibility and urgency of an archaeology of the contemporary. The visual evidence that Lutz presents is a testimony of the unhuman practices and politics as well as the many tragedies with which the La Lande landscapes around the Pas-de-Calais in Northern France are intimately entangled. An impressive example is the series of photographs capturing CS Grenades used by French security forces during the clearance of the main migrant encampment in 2016. Lutz has collected these vocal objects from the surface of a now human-devoid and ›re-naturated‹ landscape, in which only traces of provisional habitation remind us of the adversities committed at the height of the so-called ›refugee crisis‹. The grenades are pars pro toto and attest to the quasi-militarized status of the Jungle